JANINE OLIVIA

ENTERPRISES

Also by Janine Conway
(was Janine Wiggins)

Focused, Effective, Fundraising
The Trustee Handbook
Overcome Inertia
Fix Your Money, Find Your Honey

Stop Blocking Your Legacy!

Part 1

By

Janine Conway

Get out of your own way and build a legacy of success!!

Characters in this book are composites of many people with names and details changed to protect their identities.

Thanks To:

God the Father
My Lord and Savior Jesus Christ
The Precious Holy Spirit

Also, thanks to my miracle baby, Philip Ethan Wiggins, who makes this earthly life worth living and motivates me to be the best I can be. I love you!

And, finally, thanks to the amazing man God sent into my life who has encouraged me in every book, speaking engagement, and business activity. Chris Conway, you are the wind beneath my wings and I couldn't do this without your strength and support.

This Book Is Dedicated To

All of the amazing, multi-talented women in my life who inspired me to embrace my personality and use it for God's glory.

Your mentorship and friendship has sharpened me, as iron sharpeneth iron, and your legacies inspire me. Your lives are shining testimonies of God's power, grace, and mercy.

Introduction:

Over the last few years I have successfully transitioned a volunteer hobby helping people get out of debt into a solid, profitable, company that empowers individuals through financial education and financial planning.

Many coaches and mentors have guided me along this path, and all of them, no matter WHAT area of my business they were addressing, forced upon me the same conclusion:

I am my own worst enemy.

Not the man. Not the glass ceiling. Not the time constraints of being a single working mom (and, later, a married, working mother of a growing family).

ME.

Yes, there are many outside factors I have to overcome. All of us have internal and external characteristics that hinder us. We have circumstances thrust upon us. We have pasts that weren't our fault.

It's not the obstacle we face, but how we attack it.

In this book, I will share with you many of the ways *I* was blocking *my* legacy.

It is my hope that you will find yourself in my struggles, and that you will learn from them.

Please keep an open and honest mind as you read through these chapters. While they're designed to be quick, the self-reflection that accompanies each one could take some serious time and effort!

Throughout the book, you will find links to special bonuses and downloads designed to help you grow that business or ministry that has been calling you.

I sincerely hope you will contact me and let me know how this book has helped you build YOUR legacy!

You can connect with me at any time through JJConway.org or facebook.com/JJConwayORG.

Table of Contents

Chapter 1:
Ineffective Busywork

Are you DOING a lot, but getting nothing DONE?

I really didn't understand WHY I wasn't more successful! I spent many hours learning about business, working my business, networking, making new contacts, etc. Yet, years later, I wasn't getting where I wanted to go. I was only treading water!

Have you felt this way? Are you non-stop from sun-up to sun-down and feel like you have nothing to show for it at the end of the day?

Eventually, this can lead to burn-out. Or loss of faith as the family gets tired of "we're almost there" and "just one more class." Everyone wants to enjoy the reward for all of their hard work and sacrifice.

So why are so many of us overworked and underpaid? Why aren't our business flourishing like they should for the inordinate amount of time and effort we're putting in??

I offer a few reasons from my own life and the lives of my mentors:

1. Focusing on the urgent instead of the important
2. Being seduced by the Good Idea Fairy
3. Failing to get organized

The Urgent vs. the Important

Years ago, I took a wonderful class by Stephen Covey called "The 7 Habits of Highly Effective people. He used an illustration that rocked my world!

Picture 3 glass jars - one half full of sand, one half full of pebbles and one half full of big rocks.

We were told to fit the pebbles and rocks into the jar with the sand. Of course we could not do it

The facilitator finally showed us that if you start with the jar of big rocks already in place, you can more easily fit the pebbles around them and then pour in the sand around all of it. Some time-management courses add an extra step and pour in water into that showing there's yet still even more space.

This shows us that the reason we don't accomplish as much as we should, despite how worn out we are being busy, busy, busy, is because we don't first place the "big rocks" in our life.

You see, the big rocks represent those things that are most important in our lives. The pebbles represent all the not-so-important things that *feel* very important but tend to swallow up more of our time than they're wroth (phone calls, emails, etc.). Finally, the sand represents the non-urgent but appealing things that somehow drain away all of our productive time (surfing the web, TV). These non-productive and non-urgent things are often so compelling that we find ourselves taking care of them at the expense of the "big rocks."

This is not an illustration of how to get more done with less time (a big criticism of Covey's illustration).

Getting more done with less time does us no good if we don't take care of the important things!!

Let's challenge ourselves to take inventory of what's most important in our lives and our businesses. Where do we want to be 10, 20, 30 years from now? What are our family, personal, and business goals? What facets of life are important to us? Relationships? Faith? Accomplishment? Community? Material success?

If family is important to you, I might recommend constantly analyzing how the "family relationships" big rock is being scheduled in your life. Far too many who have gone before us look back and express regret for having built a legacy, yet losing their family in the process.

> If someone saw my checkbook and calendar, what would they say were my priorities this week?

Once the "big rocks" are firmly in place, then we can fill in with all the urgent things that clamor for our attention. And finally, we can fill our jar with the sandy pieces of non-productive things that we just enjoy.

I think back to this lesson whenever I feel overwhelmed taking care of email after email and phone call after phone call without any growth in outreach or profit.

The Seductive Good Idea Fairy

Chris Hogan, during a coaching event I attended, said that he and many entrepreneurs have an amazing idea every single day. They are great ideas with incredible profit potential.

So what's the problem with that?

Not all of those great ideas are needed for us to build our legacies! In fact, many of them are distractions!

This is certainly true in my own life!

In the space of one boring two hour meeting, I can come up with a great new business idea, to include marketing and business plan outlines. I'll have a rough sketch of what the website would look like, have already identified some social media outlets and a couple of friends who would be perfect ambassadors for that business.

And there was a time that every one of these great ideas would result in a week or two (or more) of me trying to implement it. After all, such greatness shouldn't be wasted, right?

Wrong!

These great ideas come to us because we are built that way. We are creative, entrepreneurial, and we see opportunity EVERYWHERE! It's in us. We almost can't help it!

Yet we must.

We must resist the constant giftings of what I call "The Good Idea Fairy" and evaluate each of these "good ideas" against our personal and business mission and vision statements.

This doesn't mean time spent indulging in these thought experiments is squandered! Not at all! I find that these excursions not only keep me from head-bobbing during useless meetings I've somehow been compelled to attend, or from falling asleep on public transit, but they also keep my mind sharp. Sometimes I run into someone needing mentoring on a business idea, and because I've previously thought about something similar, I'm in a unique position to help them.

What it means is, I evaluate all of my "good ideas" against the goals I've established for my business and my personal life. Whatever doesn't further those goals may have been an entertaining excursion, but beyond that it doesn't warrant any more of my attention, time, or money.

Organization is Boring!

You'll note a theme in the last two sections. Basically, we fall into the trap of being too busy to actually get things done when we lose sight of what's truly important in our lives.

To combat this, I'm going to suggest you do something that is very, very hard for me personally: Get organized!

Those of you who know me are laughing because you know I'm constantly losing notes because they're somewhere in one of 3 or 4 rotating notebooks (whichever one is closest when I run into a meeting) and my kitchen table looks like something of a garbage dump (Hey, all I need is a clear path to the microwave).   I get squeamish easily and don't like dirt, but life without clutter is just, well, abnormal for me.

This is not the kind of organization I'm talking about here!

Though, since I brought it up, I may as well offer some sort of solution if you suffer from "clutter-it is" like I do: my organizational skills have been greatly helped by switching to steno notebooks that fit in my purse (so I have the same one… most of the time), by purchasing an organizer to file my bills and such as they come in, and by hiring someone (no kidding) to come in and help with certain tasks.   Having her come in every other week forces me to organize (at least that often) and standardize my processes (that is, create checklists of what I do) so that she can do them for me.

What I'm really talking about here as far as organization goes, is that we must think through and plan out where we are going.

I'm talking about developing a mission and vision statement, both in our business lives and in our personal lives.   I'm talking about charting out what we want to accomplish in the next quarter, next six months, next year, next couple of years.

When we actually think through all of that (AND write it down) we are better able to plan first for our big rocks and then manage the whims of the Good Idea Fairy.

Then we won't find ourselves spending so much time on projects that don't further our goals!

Please allow me to share an example from my own life: My husband has been on radio quite a bit and has a wonderful radio voice. We've talked quite a bit about putting together a radio show. We planned it out, came up with themes, and set to buying the equipment we needed to develop quality podcasts. After about 3 weeks, I realized I was so consumed with this project that I had not progressed in building my business.

The radio show was not a bad idea! It's actually a great idea, and one that was echoed by the staff of Ramsey Solutions when I took my first financial coach training at their facility. That said, a variety radio show on relationships, Bible Study, sports, etc., might have been fun for the local area and yet netted me nothing for my financial education business. So we evaluated the idea against my goals (and his) and settled on a money-focused radio show. We still talk about controversial issues. We still talk about relationships. We even still talk about sports (sometimes). We just do so in the context of finances!

A coworker wanted me to partner with his STEM-based youth mentoring program in the schools. I agreed, as long as it could be in the context of teaching them financial life skills. Once I saw that there really wasn't much room for financial advocacy within his curriculum, I connected him with someone more applicable to his mission and divested myself of this opportunity, even though it was inspiring (and STEM is very near and dear to my heart).

So, to summarize:

We combat ineffective busywork by focusing on the important things before the urgent things, by evaluating the gifts of the "good idea fairy" against our big rocks and goals, and by getting organized with respect to where we are headed, both personally and professionally.

Pssst: Don't worry- the other chapters are MUCH shorter!

Chapter 2:
Bad Case of the Shingles

If I build it, they will come...right?

> *I built my website and social media platforms. I printed*
> *new business cards and postcards and marketing flyers. I*
> *made magnets to giveaway, and waited for the customers*
> *who would soon beat down my door. Only they never did!*

Many of us have fallen into the "Field of Dreams" trap. Field of Dreams is a movie about a man who hears a voice repeatedly saying, "If you build it, he will come" and interprets this to mean build a baseball field in the cornfields behind his house. He's about to lose the farm, since the crops have been replaced by the field, and everyone's beginning to think he's crazy. Ghosts of some great Chicago White Sox players come to play ball, plus the ghost of his dad. The resulting cult attraction amongst ghost-chasers and baseball aficionados, the ending implies, will bring in enough money to save the farm.

The key phrase in this movie, "If you build it, he will come" has been usurped in many an inspirational speech.

If we will just build our website, business, and set up a quaint little office in just the right part of town, then surely the customers will come flocking to our business! After all, we offer some amazing products and services and people would be crazy not to use them!

I truly believe that. I truly believe that if you are reading this book you either already offer an amazing service or product, or that you soon will!

It's just that we can't set up shop, hang out a "shingle" with our name on it outside the door, and expect people to come flocking in.

Building a business takes work. It takes relationship-building. It takes getting out there and spreading our name, our brand, our company, until a critical mass of people are clamoring for US!

Too often, we spend an inordinate amount of time on setting up shop rather than building brand awareness and loyalty.

Maybe it's just me? Am I the only one who will spend 2 hours organizing my desk: placing the stapler, pens, and paper clips "just so," decorating with just the right touches to make my future clients feel at home, painstakingly selecting the right air freshener and flowers, rearranging the furniture 20+ times... but never actually getting down to business?

Am I the only one who spent 3 months trying to perfect a website, agonizing for days over one tiny blip somewhere instead of getting out there and driving traffic TO the website? And then, once it was set up, I couldn't understand why no one was visiting. No one was signing up for my newsletter. No one was buying my books. Huh? I built it! They should have come!!

After whining to one of my coaches about the lack of paying clients, I received a very important lesson:

The minute you go into business for yourself, you become a salesperson.

No, no, no! I'm not built for sales. I'm too blunt, too serious, and too, um, ME, to be in sales! I resisted his message until I realized I was paying him good money to help me take this business to the next level and I'd better listen to what he has to say!

He outlined for me the following action plan:
1. Do admin work (website, emailing, filing, etc.) during times outside of "normal business hours" when you can't realistically meet with clients anyway.
2. During business hours, either you're meeting with clients or out doing "client attraction" activities such as seminars, marketing, networking, and finding new contacts (and employer groups).

That's it. Sounds simple, doesn't it? I found it harder than expected, especially since I was building up my business while still active duty military.

I didn't have much in the way of flexible schedule, so back then my business building was mostly relegated to lunch breaks. The switch in mindset from doing the admin work during those sparse breaks to doing it early morning or late night freed me up during the day to make contacts with new people and take virtual appointments.

Most of my financial education business is virtual, conducted in the evenings or during lunches now.

Because my time was limited, I adapted the "action plan" to fit even better into my crazy world. Everyone says you should get up an hour early to get more done. That just wasn't going to happen for me! This busy single mom already shortchanged sleep on the regular. I needed something that would be consistent for months, if needed. What I didn't need was a mind-blowing action plan that would fall by the wayside after a few weeks because it was too unwieldy for me to do every day.

So I came up with this "1 hour Prospecting Daily Admin" plan I developed to help me meet the first part of my coach's action plan:

1 hour Prospecting Daily Admin:

1. *20 minutes: answer social media / emails (handle and file NOW)*
2. *5 min: Post to known networking sites*
3. *5 min: Search out new networking sites*
4. *5 min: Research a new business to reach out to their EAP or HR director*
5. *5 min: Contact that HR or EAP*
6. *10 min: planning / updating calendar*
7. *10 min: random needed tasks / overflow time*

- *RESIST the urge to keep going - have other work to get done!!!*
- *With "searching new opportunities" if I do this every day, I should have a good collection built up by end of the month. It shouldn't take long to market electronically once I get my scripts built.*

I saved the results from each day's prospecting (seeking out new sites to sell to or network with) in a word document, and my list of social media and other potential avenues for marketing really grew!

My biggest challenge was make sure I resisted the urge to keep going past the timelines prescribed. You see, I would get to posting on some sites, and get sucked into "just one more" until I ran out of time completely.

What I like about this kind of model is that most of us can find an hour in our schedule by cutting down some of the non-essentials such as TV, internet surfing, and addictive video game apps.

While I must still make time for product creation, client management, and actual financial analysis, this 1 hr daily model still helps me find new clients. I am now at the point where people who have never used my services are so comfortable with my expertise that they're referring me to their friends and family.

The important takeaway from this chapter is that it's not enough to physically build a business. In order to establish our legacy, we must also get out there and sell ourselves to potential customers. Even when our business becomes so established that referrals bring in more than enough income, we must continually budget some of our time toward prospecting for and selling to new customers.

Chapter 3:
Follow-Up Follies

Ain't nobody got time for dat!

I hated networking! It seemed like such a waste of time! You spend an hour or two at a networking event, another hour or two putting everyone into your contacts database, and then NOTHING! No leads, no customers, no profit! Just spam from people trying to sell me on their business opportunity! Why am I wasting my time?

Whoo-Chile! I have beeeeen there! I am not a networker by nature. I am not the warm, friendly personality who lights up a room when she walks in. I hire those warm personalities to make up for my directness, my down-to-business demeanor, and my overall disdain for frivolities that waste time I could be spending with my kids.

So when one of my mentors hammered into me that I really needed to network more, I dug in my heels! Well, I'm glad he prodded me because in uncovering why I hated networking, he revealed some very fundamental mistakes I was making! These mistakes were costing me my business!

1. Ineffective networking
2. Lack of follow-up
3. Poor client relationship management

Ineffective networking

It was bad enough that I didn't' like networking, but when I did go to a networking session, I was doing it all wrong!

One of my mentors, an experienced financial coach, pinpointed it during our first session: "You lack confidence," he said. "You know your stuff, and one-on-one with a client you really perform well. But you get in front of a room of potential clients and act like you're not worthy to be there."

That really stung.

Because the truth hurts!

I had to address that confidence issue because it not only impacted potential clients but also other professionals with whom I'd want to share referrals.

Lack of follow-up

Mark Emerson, in his article, "The Profit Is In The Follow Up," outlines some eye-opening stats regarding follow-up:

- 48% of sales people never follow up with a prospect.
- 25% follow up just once.
- 12% make contact three times.
- Only 10% follow up with a prospect more than three times.

Then he goes on to say:

- 2% of sales are made on first contact
- 3% on second contact
- 5% on the third
- 10% on the fourth follow up
- 80% of sales are made on the fifth to twelfth follow up

I guess that means we'd better do something with those piles of business cards in crazy places all over the office. Oh, you know the ones: They're from the last 7 networking events we attended, and we keep saying we're going to follow-up one of these days. That day never comes and soon we're overwhelmed with cards from the next event. We don't feel too bad about it because, at least, they're in separate piles and we remember what event they came from. Right??

Ok, so if 80% of sales are made on the 5th to 12th follow-up, and we're not really following up at all, is it any wonder that we don't have sales like we should?

Our products and services are part of an amazing legacy we're building not only for our families but for those who we serve in the marketplace. We've just got to get them to see this! And we do that by following up. A lot.

Follow-up can take on many forms: telephone, email, snail mail, text message, door knocking (surprisingly), social media, and even ad campaigns (virtual or physical).

"If you don't have a reason to follow up," one mentor told me, "Then create one!" He was right! By creating seminars and events, I was able to effectively market those community benefit events along with my business.

There are many "follow-up programs" out there, from once-a-month post cards featuring a seasonal tip and your business information, to more advanced marketing campaigns that encompass all of the forms listed above for a particular market segment. I encourage you to search the internet to find a strategy suitable for your business and personality.

Poor client relationship management

So you've networked, and you've put everyone you met into your fabulous email marketing program. You're ready to do your daily follow-up and you reach for the notebook where you jotted down notes about them. Only it's not there, and they've answered the phone! You can't remember anything about them! What do you do?

Well, if you have a good client relationship management system, you simply pull up their account and read all the notes you've captured about them and your interactions. A lot of companies now use customer relationship management systems (CRMs) to store information about each time a customer calls into service. This is why, when you give the customer service rep your account number, she can pull up the history of conversations. Because each person who interacts with you is supposed to summarize those dealings in the system.

If you don't have a good CRM, you might find yourself winging it like I did after a move where I couldn't find the boxes with all of my client files. This is because we had to move in the files, and you already heard above, I tend to have a "piles everywhere" problem (just pray for me!) combined with a "get round to it" problem.

Your CRM can simply be file folders for each client, or you can spend big money to implement an electronic system.

My favorite CRM, which I'll decline to name in this book, was designed for real estate agents. It costs a fair amount each month, and I feel the cost is worth it because you can develop checklists for every type of individual you put into the system. If I'm putting in a fellow veteran, I select veteran and system runs my checklist against her account from then on. She'll get several auto responder emails -one per week for a month- and then once a month the checklist will bring up some military-related fact and then ping me to draft an email to the "veterans" group. If I meet moms from my son's school, I input them into the "moms" group and those auto responders will be sent and that checklist will activate. Every time I log in, the system will tell me what steps on the various checklists should be accomplished that day, so I don't even have to keep track of it. It will tell me if there's any birthdays (so I can fire off a quick note or even send a physical card). It will tell me if I need to follow up with a financial client or a real estate broker, and as long as I've built proper checklists into the CRM, it ensures I don't let slip a valuable opportunity to reach out to potential and existing clients .

Chapter 4:
We Do It All - Just Not Well

We're so well rounded, we're pointless!

> *We've been gifted with a HUGE vision and I'm not gonna limit myself to just one aspect! We're launching full steam ahead with all 7 of our focus areas and it's gonna be amazing!!*

I've heard this sentiment more times than I care to admit! I fell into the trap at one time myself. It makes me sad when a young entrepreneur says something along these lines to me. 9 times out of 10, a year later they will have accomplished nothing beyond their website and facebook page. Those will be stale, because they had so many programs they were trying to launch that none of them ever got off the ground!

PR Consultant Leila Lewis said it best:

> Do one thing and do it well. Don't confuse your potential customer and dilute your brand. If you aren't good at everything you claim to do, it will hurt your profits and your reputation.

Be memorable by being you and offering your best products and services. If you do too much they may not remember what it is you do and why they should hire you.

We get so excited about the vision growing within us that we find ourselves taking on way too much! Essentially, we spread ourselves so thin we become translucent, and potential clients see right through us to the bold, specialized, expert standing behind us.

There are natural areas where businesses can dovetail. For example, as a financial planner, I found that becoming a Realtor ® was a logical next step because real estate investing figures heavily into my investment strategy.

Several of my previous businesses have nothing to do with finance. Let's see: I've created and sold a web design and webhosting business. An online children's boutique, financial education, real estate investing. I've taught at Air University. I've been a missionary in South America and head trustee for several churches (military scientist- moved often), and still minister. I used to teach fitness classes, too!

Doesn't reading all that just exhaust you??

I used to give that litany of all the things I did in my life, thinking it would impress people into hiring me. All it did was either make them think I was totally pompous or make them think I was a "jack of all trades, master of none." To differentiate ourselves in the marketplace in today's environment of overnight YouTube sensations where anyone can learn to do anything through a Google search, we MUST bring extreme value to the table. When our clients interact with us, they must feel they are getting an exceptional value. They must feel like they are making a solid investment in themselves, by engaging us to serve them.

Some feel their legacy will be hindered by focusing on one or two areas as they're getting started. After-all, for someone who feels called to serve on a global level hearing "play in the township first" sounds stifling!

You don't have to set aside your dream, your vision, or your legacy! Indeed, throttling back early in the process and focusing on the mastery of one aspect at a time can be **very** healthy for an upstart business.

As Gary Keller says in his book, *The One Thing*, "Focus on the ONE thing that's most important. And when that's accomplished, focus on the next ONE thing."

Let me give you a real-world example of how taking it one step at a time can lead to an AMAZING LEGACY!

If you've never heard of Jaspen Boothe, please do look her up. Military member who was dealt the double blow of cancer plus losing her home to Hurricane Katrina, this amazing woman founded Final Salute, Inc. to address the lack of available support services for homeless female veterans.

I first heard of her and her organization in 2012 when an old friend competed in the inaugural Ms. Veteran America competition. My friend also competed in 2013, and urged me to give it a go in 2014. I placed as a finalist and the event was life-changing for me. The mentoring I received was invaluable! And I learned, from watching Ms. Boothe build her organization, that the best way to make something last is to build it one solid step at a time. Founded in 2010, Final Salute, Inc. began providing financial assistance and housing programs, to assist homeless female veterans in 2011. In 2012, the Ms. Veteran America competition was established to raise funds and awareness for the effort. In 2013, the "Stand Up for Women Vets" event, which provides women veterans with free professional clothes, free makeovers, and free headshots, was created. In 2014, Final Salute Inc. launched a comprehensive awareness campaign that resulted in Ms. Boothe being honored by Oprah, People Magazine, CNN, and participating (in 2015) in a White House summit on Veterans Affairs.

I look at the incredible impact Ms. Boothe is having on, not just homeless women veterans, but the entire world, and it all started with one step. Each year they've added on, and each project has been successful. Her legacy is still expanding, and I suspect had she tried to do ALL of this from day one, she never would have been able to launch!

Please consider breaking your legacy-sized vision into discrete manageable portions, and tackle them one at a time.

It's like eating an elephant: you can only do so one bite at a time!

Chapter 5:
The Never-ending Quest

Unique (or Perfect) Enough Never Is!

I'm going to launch. As soon as I finish _____ project. And after I take _____class. And after I tweak my website. And after I participate in Guru X's mentoring program. And... And... And...

There are so many ways we block our legacy in this category!

And I truly mean "we" here because I'm super guilty as charged. It was one of the hardest business lessons I learned the year I transitioned from volunteer financial coaching for fee-for service financial planning. You'll learn about the #1 hardest thing for me to accept in the follow-on volume *Stop Blocking Your Legacy, Part 2.*

There are times when we legitimately seek time making sure our business is unique enough to capture an adequate market. We need to differentiate ourselves and it's wise to spend some foundational time doing that research.

What blocks our legacy is constantly tweaking and improving things that either don't really need "improving" or are such minimal return on investment that the time spent tweaking would be better spent elsewhere.

Some of us spend so much effort trying to differentiate ourselves that we never actually get ourselves OUT there!

Perhaps we've been incapacitated by "Analysis of Paralysis," where we spend so much time analyzing a situation that we never actually make a decision about how to handle it. We keep playing situations over and over in our mind, and seeking out new information because we're so scared of making the wrong choice!

Perhaps we still haven't discovered that "Perfection is the enemy of good enough," and that by continuing to pursue perfection, we are losing valuable time while our competitors are taking action to secure their profits.

Again, we want to be professional in establishing our business. That means taking time to fully research and develop a business plan, as well as a marketing plan. That means testing your niche and researching your chosen audience to ensure they are both interested in your service (or product) AND are able to afford your rates.

The trouble comes when we fall into the "must be unique" and "must be perfect" traps outlined above.

Throwing Out The Baby With the Bathwater

Sometimes, we just automatically assume the old sales techniques are passé, and that what we need now is a new strategy for a new world order.

That's exactly how I felt. This was the age of internet! They didn't even have internet (or personal computers) when I was a kid, so surely those old- fashioned sales techniques are useless today. It's all social media, baby! We don't need no stinkin' door-knockin'! Bring on the facebook and twitter! I'll buy an ad and the crowds will flock in.

First, see Chapter 2: Bad Case of the Shingles for a discussion on why "If you build it they will come" can be a dangerous attitude to have about when building a business.

Secondly, while today's smart marketers will certainly maximize social media, many sectors enjoy significant profit from the "old techniques." Mailing campaigns (email or physical), door knocking (a shock to me!), promotional giveaways, and great taglines/jingles/slogans are still key ways to attract customers and clients.

There are certainly those marketing techniques that just aren't relevant anymore. For example, when was the last time you picked up a phone book? However, in our search for the most cost-effective bang for our marketing buck, we must be careful to resist the urge to "improve" what's worked for others until you've gained some experience making it work for YOU. Find someone who is successful at what you want to do, and then benchmark (a fancy word for "copy") their strategy.

Or, Is It An Avoidance Mechanism?

How long has it been since you've established your niche? How long has it been since you did the research, established your company, bought your web-name, and printed your business cards?

Let's talk about our quest to make our businesses as unique as we are. I mean, after all: we're fabulous! We've got style, moxie, rhythm, and a host of other traits that make us amazing. We know we've got it going on, and our businesses are going to be magnificent! We know we'll rock this!

Or do we?

Is our incessant pursuit for uniqueness in our professional approach really about our business? Or is it about our own lack of confidence?

Before you answer, please consider the following questions:

Why are so many of us continually taking class after class and coaching program after coaching program? Why do we feel that "just one more" will hold the key to unlock the mysteries of our success?

> I remember it like it was yesterday: My very first real estate investor's club meeting. I was fascinated by stories of wealth gained through flipping houses and the sheer number of people in the room (over 200). My wonder and excitement quickly disappeared, however, when person after person had the same story as one man who'd spent over $80,000 in real estate training materials. He waxed poetic about what an amazing education he'd received through the group. Imagine my surprise at his response when I asked him how many properties he owned: "None yet, but I think after buying the course they talked about today I'll be ready for my first deal."

That gentleman didn't *really* need one more course in flipping homes. What he needed was a solid dose of confidence, whether that came through a mentor or (as is the case for many a real estate investor) just jumping into the water and DOING IT.

Are you really trying to finalize the last few details on your unique business? Does the fear of making costly mistakes prevent you from moving forward? Or, have you been conditioned by past events (naysayers) that you can't really experience success?

Are you scared to death that success might actually find you, and take away every excuse for living an ordinary life?

Are you subconsciously concerned that your success might so convict your family and friends that you'll lose them?

These are questions only you can answer.

To summarize:

Many of us block our legacies by continually using little excuses to keep us from excelling. We might seek so much to be unique that we dismiss what's working for someone else in our field. We might lack the confidence to fully embrace the legacy burning deep within us.

Combat this never-ending quest by establishing the niche that makes YOU unique, and then apply proven sales and client generation techniques to that niche. Resist the urge to "improve" what's worked for others until you've gained some experience making it work for YOU!

In Conclusion:

I truly hope this book has been a blessing to you. We've talked about 5 key ways that aspiring entrepreneurs block their legacies and we've provided you, the reader, with real world examples of how you can overcome and avoid these traps!

I sincerely hope you will contact me and let me know how this book has helped you build YOUR legacy!

You can connect with me at any time through JJConway.org or facebook.com/JJConwayORG.

Blessings,

JJ

Epilogue:

What Will Part 2 Cover?

Like what you've read?
Come back for another helping!

This book focused on the 5 key traps that block the legacies of aspiring entrepreneurs.

Part 2 will cover 5 more traps, these being from the financial realm, that degrade our personal AND business legacies.

For a FREE download of

"Daily Affirmations"

Please subscribe to our newsletter

At

http://eepurl.com/buLQQj

And Be Sure To Visit

http://www.jjconway.org/index.php